Poems from the Garden of my Heart

*An invitation to the fellowship
of His presence*

JEAN MATTSON

authorHOUSE®

AuthorHouse™
1663 Liberty Drive
Bloomington, IN 47403
www.authorhouse.com
Phone: 1-800-839-8640

First published by AuthorHouse 1/17/2011

ISBN: 978-1-4567-2088-9 (e)
ISBN: 978-1-4567-2089-6 (sc)

Library of Congress Control Number: 2011900298

Printed in the United States of America

Any people depicted in stock imagery provided by Thinkstock are models, and such images are being used for illustrative purposes only. Certain stock imagery © Thinkstock.

This book is printed on acid-free paper.

Forward

My Mom's poems are so timely in these uncertain times in which we live. A re-occuring theme throughout <u>Poems From the Garden of My Heart</u> is the hope, strength, peace, grace and love of God.

"What an awesome thing that You, the King of Kings should dwell in my inner being...I know that you are changing me into Your very likeness." Because "all that I am...comes from You, Lord"..."It is not about what I can do, but what You, Lord, can do through me." Through God, we are made to be, indeed, more than conquerors in life.

Of course as humans we experience despairing moments. "When there is darkness on every side And your fears do not subside When your heart is filled with grief And from pain there is no relief Rest assured of His great love."

"Though I cannot see above the clouds, my Father sees the whole picture. Everything is alright from His view." "For now all that He requires is (for me) to live one moment at a time. Oh, to live that moment in the light of eternity."

In conclusion, reading <u>Poems From the Garden of My Heart</u> has impressed upon me that having God as the foundation of my life makes me unbreakable. My Mom is one of the strongest people I know. I thank God that He chose my Mom for me. I pray my Mom's heartfelt poems will richly bless and speak to your heart, as they have mine

by Lynelle Mattson

Acknowledgements

I want to give praise, honor and glory to the Lord Jesus, my Savior, Guide, and Friend for His mercy in allowing me to share these poems which are the expressions of my faith and hope in Him

I want to thankLynelle Mattson, Kathi Crissman and Nancy Claborn for theirhours of work in editing, for their encouragement and prayers which have meant so much to me. A special thanks to Lynelle for writing the Forward.

I want to thank Brandon Battle for all of his help in the technology of my computer,as well asassisting with the sizing and resolutionof the pictures.

I want to thank the Author House staff for their great assistance and detailed instruction in making it possible for me to publish this book.

Contents

Worship and Thanksgivng   1

Eternity   17

Salvation   27

Living in Christ   43

Dedication   53

Encouragement   69

Introduction

God can speak through poetry. In the Bible the Books of Job, Psalms, Proverbs, Ecclesiasties and Song of Solomon are known as books of poetry.Poetry often expresses the way one feels deep in his heart. David, the shepherd boy who later became king of Israel, learned at an early age to worship and praise the Lord. His songs are written in the Psalms. Later when he went through hard trials, David was able to trust God because he knew Him in a personal way.

Adam and Eve had unbroken fellowship with God. When sin entered into the world that relationship was broken. Can a human being still experience the presence of God?We cannot experience His physical presence; however, He has opened the way to an even deeper relationship.

God has restored that fellowship by giving His Son, the Lord Jesus Christ, to die for our sins. When we accept Jesus as Lord and Saviour, He gives us a new spirit, His spirit who dwells in our hearts. Our new spirit delights to fellowship with God, our Heavenly Father. These poems come from times offellowship with Him. I invite you into the fellowship of His presence. As you read these poems may you be drawn to Jesus.

Worship and Thanksgiving

"Oh, sing to the Lord a new song
Sing to the Lord all the earth."
Psalm 96:1

Our God Reigns

Our God reigns, He reigns, He reigns
He reigns in majesty; He is the King of Glory
He reigns in victory; He is risen forever more
He reigns in purity; He only is holy
He reigns in wisdom; He is the Creator
He reigns in justice; He is judge of the world
The LORD our God reigns; He reigns in righteousness
He reigns over all the earth; He reigns over land and sea
He reigns over all the heaven; Angelic hosts obey Him
He reigns over all the universe: In Him all things consist
He reigns above all evil powers; Triumphant over all

His Name is King of Kings
His Name is Lord of Lords
He is the Great I Am
He is the Mighty Counselor
He is the Prince of Peace
HIS NAME IS JESUS

Thank You, Lord

How can I thank you, Lord, for Your love for me?
You have ransomed me from the enemy.
A thousand, million years and in all eternity
I could never repay the debt I owe to Thee.
This life on earth goes by like the blinking of an eye;
Compared to your greatness I'm a dot in the sky.
But you have given me significance
Nothing in my life is happenstance
My steps you have ordained
with good works to glorify Your Name.

Deep Within My Heart

Deep within my heart, within my soul
I hear You calling, calling, Lord
Deep within my heart, within my soul
I hear You calling" Come and worship me."

Deep within my heart, within my soul
I have a longing, I have a longing
Deep within my heart, within my soul
I have a longing to worship You.

Deep within my heart, within my soul
I feel the breeze of Your Spirit flowing
Cleansing, healing,making me whole
Deep within my heart, within my soul.

I Applaud You

I applaud You, Lord for all You have done
I applaud You, Lord for all You are
I applaud You, Lord for You are worthy
Worthy of all applause

I applaud You, Lord for leaving heaven's glory
Being willing to lay aside Your honor
For humbling Yourself to be clothed in humanity
For living a life in obedience to the Father

I applaud You, Lord for defeating the tempter
In every type of trial and testing
Not giving in to worldly fame or pressure
Using the Word You were the Victor

I applaud You, Lord for the life You lived
King of Kings, yet You had no pillow for Your head
With the Father's blessing the multitude You fed
Going forth healing, setting free those who were bound

I applaud You, Lord for going to the cross
For paying the awful cost of my sin and shame
For bearing my sickness and pain
You cried, "It is finished", redemption was complete

I applaud You, Lord, You arose up from the grave
Of the true church You are the Head
Coming soon, You will be crowned
I now applaud You, Lord of Lords and King of Kings

It's All About Praising Jesus

In every accomplishment
In every joy fulfilled
In every word of wisdom
May my focus be

It's all about praising You, Lord
It's all about loving You
It's all about worshipping You
With all of my heart

In this world of sin and strife
Trials may come and trials may go
And when at times I'm feeling low
Help me remember this

It's all about praising You, Lord
It's all about loving You
It's all about worshipping You
With all of my heart

Jesus, I Desire You

Jesus, I desire You,
I really desire You.
I desire to worship You,
I desire to honor You.

I desire to walk and talk with You
to tell You all about my day;
I want You to show me the way.
I desire to tell You all about
my joys and success,
my failures and heartaches, too

But there is more.....

I desire to listen to Your voice
To know what makes You sad,
To know what makes You glad.
I desire to follow You
To know the fellowship of Your pain
To seek no earthly gain

How Can I Not Love You, Lord?

How can I not love You, Lord?
You gave your life for me.
How can I not love You
with all my heart, and strength and soul?
You have come to make me whole.

How can I not love You, Lord?
You rose up from the dead
In You I have the victory
From self and sin
You have come to set me free.

How can I not worship You
Bowing in humility?
You who are the King of Kings
How can I not honor You?
Of You my soul must sing.

A New Song

Lord, you gave me a new song
I will trust You in the storm and wind
when my path is rough or plain
for You know my name

You surround me with Your love
You encompass my way
You will never lead astray
I will trust You day by day

I will glorify Your name
to You honor will I bring
Of Your love my soul will sing
I acknowledge You as King

You Are My Song

You are my victory, You are my song
In You is forgiveness when I do wrong
You are my hope, You are my joy
You are my peace that none can destroy

You are my purpose, You are my life
In You is no darkness, only pure light
You are my glory, You are my King
All day long Your praise I sing

Joyful

In the stillness of the morning
Before the day has begun
I am walking, thinking of my Lord
In the stillness of the day

If He was here beside me
Like the children I would run
and leap and shout for joy
I would pick a bouquet of flowers
I would look up into His face
Filled with such glory and grace

Yet He is closer than beside me
He now lives within me
He speaks to my spirit saying,
"Child rejoice"

Joyful expectation, joyful expectation
These two words come to my mind
In nothing I shall be ashamed
of Jesus Christ my Lord
He has run the race before me;
His hope is now within me
His promises will not fail

Lord, You Are Worthy

LORD, You are worthy,
Worthy in wisdom
Worthy in righteousness
Worthy in purity
Worthy in faithfulness
LORD, You are worthy
Worthy as Creator
Worthy as Sustainer
Worthy as Redeemer
Worthy as Judge

Worship In Spirit

With my spirit I will seek the Lord
With my spirit I will worship
With my spirit I will obey His voice
In my spirit is Your righteousness

By Your Spirit You reveal the hidden things
That my heart cannot see
By Your Spirit from all bondage
You will set me free

I will dance and shout and praise Your name
Let the heavens hear, the earth be glad
The Spirit reigns within my heart
The kingdom of our God is come

It Is You, O Lord

It is You, O Lord, Who gives me eyes to see
It is You Who gives me ears to hear
It is You Who gives me breath to breathe
In You alone is life indeed.

It is You, O Lord, Who makes my mind to think
From You comes wisdom, power and strength
But one thing alone You have left for me to do
You have given me a will to choose

Will I give You glory and praise?
Will I follow You all of my days?
Or
Will my eyes be closed to see what You are doing?
Will my ears be dull To hear Your voice?
Will my heart not understand Your ways?

I lay my life before You, My ambitions and dreams
I give to You, Your will I choose
By Your grace I will obey
By Your Spirit I will say, "Yes, LORD,
Youare my life-I'll walk with You, today.

Hands

When I lift my hands in praise to You
I lift my heart in surrender to Your will
When I lift my hands in worship to Your Name
Then I come in humility, not shame
Not ashamed to call You Lord
Not ashamed to glorify Your name

When I lift my hands in time of need
As a little child lifts up his hands for his father
to carry him when he can go no further
I lift up my hands and cry,
"Father, I need you in the storms of life, "Carry me,
Hide me in the bosom of Your love"

Stretch out your hands to the Savior
Let go of your own righteous deeds
Stretch out your hands to the One
Who can bring salvation to your soul

Stretch out your hands in humility
Let go pride and self sufficiency
Stretch out your hands to the one
Who is sufficient to meet every need.-

Eternity

*"Before the mountains were
brought forth, or ever you
formed the earth and the world,
even from everlasting to
everlasting, You are God."*
Psalm 90:1

The End Of The Way

When I come to the end of the day
And enter the day that never ends
I want to hear Him say, "Well done
Your course you have run
Come enter into the place
I have prepared for you"

When I come to the end of the day
And enter the day that never ends
There will be no night, Jesus is the light
There will be no sin, all will be pure within
No sickness will abide, Nor sorrow nor fear
He will wipe away each tear

What a wondrous, wondrous life
When I come to the end of the day
And enter the day that never ends

Ready

Ready to meet You
Looking forward to seeing Your face
Looking to neither right nor left
Being distracted with nothing less
Than obeying Your voice;
Your love pouring out
Through my hands and feet
Giving bread to those
Who have nothing to eat

Jesus are You foremost in my thoughts?
To please You, Let it be the goal of my heart,
To hear Your voicesay, "Well done"
Be all that really matters.
Let Your love permeate my being
So all that others are seeing
Is the likeness of Your image
Through my life.

My Mansion In The Sky

This old house is fading away,
This old house is getting weary every day
But God is preparing a house in the heavens
A house that will not fade away
A house by the streets of gold,
That will never grow old

I'll leave behind all sickness and pain,
All sorrow and shame
I'll leave behind all fear and sadness,
All will be joy and gladness
Famine and war will be heard of no more
When I arrive on that golden shore

But my mansion in the sky
Will be nothing in comparison
To the presence of my Lord
To look upon Him who died for me
How awesome that will be!

Could Be Any Day Now

Could be any day now
The Lord will come to receive His own
Could be any day now
The clouds will part the trumpet will sound
Could be any day now
We will leave this world behind

Oh, glory, hallelujah
What a meeting in the sky
Do you know it is drawing nigh?
Is your heart prepared?
With others
Jesus have you shared?

In a moment, in the twinkling of an eye,
He will appear to take me home
Are you ready for that meeting in the sky?
ForHis coming does your heart sigh?
Oh, glorious day

I'm looking up, looking up for the Saviour
Looking up, looking up for my King
Looking for the Lover of my soul
And to gaze on His face everyday
That will be glory for me

Destination: heaven

It's more than just a place
I can hear heaven calling
Come up hither to the Lamb
I can hear the voice of Jesus
He is the great I Am

He is calling all His children
Who are longing to be there
Coming home to glory
To see my Heavenly Bridegroom
The Lover of my soul

I can hear the heavenly anthems
Singing praise to His dear Name
I can hear the trumpet sounding
All the saved of all ages shouting
King of Kings and Lord of Lords

Waiting

In quietness
The stillness of the night
Only the tick of a clock
Children snuggling safe beneath the quilts
The light of the lantern shines down the path
Suddenly, the sound of footsteps.....
His hand upon the doorknob
FATHER'S HOME

Hopefully, with anticipation,
Expectancy is felt in the air,
New responsibility, the time is near
Suddenly, a cry is heard......
NEW LIFE is brought forth

Watching,
Working,
Walking by faith,
Willing to suffer,
Willing to weep,
Suddenly, the trumpet sounds.......
THE LORD APPEARS

Every Moment

Every moment makes up hours
Every hour makes up days
Every day makes up weeks
Every week makes up months
Every month makes up years

And so on, until the end of time
But there is eternity
God lives in eternity
Right now all He requires is
to live one moment at a time
Oh to live that moment
in the light of Eternity

Salvation

"For God so loved the world that He gave His only begotten Son that whoever believes in Him should not perish but have everlasting life." John 3: 16

When Jesus Passed By

When Jesus passed by......
He called men to follow Him
They put their fishing nets aside
In His work they would abide

When Jesus passed by
He saw Levi sitting at the gate
To follow Jesus he put aside
all earthy gain
Eternal life he would obtain

When Jesus passed by
A blind man received his sight
His spiritual eyes could also see
That Jesus was the Son of God

When Jesus passed by
He stopped the funeral procession
For the grieving He had compassion
And raised the dead to live again

When Jesus passed by
A woman reached out
Touched the hem of His garment
And was made whole

When Jesus passed by
He saw Zaccheus up in the tree
He saw his repentant heart
And from sin he was set free

Who Can This Be?

Who can this be, Who stilled the waters?
Who can this be, Who calmed the sea?
Who can this be, that the winds obey Him?
Who can this be? Who can this be?

Who can this be, Who touched the leper?
Who can this be, Who raised the dead?
Who can this be, Who the demons dread?
Who can this be? Who can this be?

Who can this be, Who opened blind eyes?
Who can this be, Who healed the deaf?
Who can this be, Who loosed the mute tongue
Who can this be? Who can this be?

Who can this be, Who walked on water?
Who can this be, Who fed the multitude?
Who can this be, Who has all authority?
Who can this be? Who can this be?

This one is JESUS, The Son of God
Who gave His life upon the cross
To save us from eternal loss
That we might an entrance gain
Before the Father's throne

This one is JESUS, Prince of Peace
Who came to set us freefrom stress
To be partakers of His Holiness
That we might have deliverance
From every sin that hinders us

This one is JESUS, the Lord of Lords
Who is coming again in victory
To receive His own up to His throne
That He might in His saints be glorified
Beholding Him in all of His beauty

The One Gift

I could give You clothes, they someday would be worn
I could give You toys, they someday would be broken
I could give You candy, it soon would be eaten
I could give You money, it soon would be spent
I could give You books, they soon would be read
I could give You pets, they too will grow old and die
Nothing that I give you in this world will last

There is one gift above all gifts
The gift of having Your sins forgiven
The gift of knowing You shall reach heaven
The gift of God's Spirit living within
Enabling You to overcome sin
That gift is God's dear Son,
For the victory He has won

I offer you God's gift today
There is no way that You can pay
The Lord Jesus Christ has paid the price
It does not depend on whether
You are naughty or nice
By faith believe Jesus died for You and rose again
Receive Him into Your heart and gain new life
It is my prayer this Christmas day
You will not turn the Savior away

Return

Come, come, come unto Me
Come, come, return unto Me
I hear the voice of the Father
calling, calling, calling
Saying, "Come, come,
Come home to roam no more
Come, come, return unto my love

I see Your love expressd
in Your Son's arms outstretched
Forgiveness He is offering,
A robe of righteousness
The angels will shout glory, glory
A child has come home,
No more to roam

I am coming closer, closer,
Closer to Your love, closer to
Your arms outstretched
Closer to Your heart
I accept your matchless grace,
I will look upon Your face
I am coming closer every day,

I have waited oh so long
For You to fill my heart with song
Nothing in this world compares
to my Father's loving care
And the glory He will share
with those who answer the call
To crown Him King and Lord of all

Have You Met Jesus?

Have You met Jesus as you walk along life's way?
Have you experienced His touch upon your soul?
Do you know that He can make you whole?
He can wash away your sin
Make you pure and clean within.

Have you met Jesus? Have you seen His face?
Do you know that It is filled with mercy and grace?
When you come to Him in faith,
He will not turn you away.
Come to Him today

Someday Jesus will be appearing
for those who His voice
have been hearing
Today is the day of salvation,
for those of every nation.

If I was walking down the path and
met Jesus coming my way, what
would my reaction be? Would I
recognize His voice?Would I
shun Him out of fear or draw near?
Would I bow in sweetsurrender?

Do You Hear?

Do you hear the Savior calling, calling, calling?"
Do you hear the Saviour calling,"Come to me?"
With outstretched ams I'm waiting, Come as you are
Come and let us reason together, though your sins
Are as scarlet, they shall be as snow
Though they be red like crimson, they shall be as wool

Come all you who are weary, and I will give you rest
You who are heavy laden with burdens to bear
Come to the cross and leave your burden there
Come you who are thirsty, drink of the water of life
Drink from My cup which never will run dry
My spirit springing up in you, an everlasting supply"

Hear the Master calling, calling, "Come and follow Me
Leave the world behind you, My disciple be
Willing to go where My footsteps lead,
On rocky mountain pathways seeking My sheep
Or in some lowly place abide, knowing
I will never leave your side."

The Bridegroom will be calling "Come,
Come to the wedding feast,
Come, for all things are ready"
Will you hear His voice?
Will your heart rejoice?
Will you answer His call?

Bound By Love

What is it that has a grip on you
That you cannot do what you want to do?
Set your eyes on the Man of Calvary
He will set you completely free

Are you shackled with selfishness or pride
And fears that will not subside?
Jesus is the truth, the life, the way
Cast all your cares on Him today

Let Him bind up your broken heart
By His Word the enemy must depart
He has borne your grief and pain,
He will cleanse you from sin's stain
He has bound His heart to you with cords of love
He will send the Comforter from above

Remembrance

I remember as You broke the bread
You said, "This is My body
which is broken for you"
I remember the stripes on Your back
And by Your stripes I am healed

I remember as You took the cup
You said, "This cup is
the new covenant in My blood"
God's cup of wrath was poured out
My sins are forever in the
sea of God's forgetfulness

I remember as You spoke the words,
"It is finished," the fulfillment of
all righteousness was done
The temple curtain was rent in two
The way to the Father was opened

I remember Your hands and feet
were nailed to the cross
we shall know You
By the nail prints in Your hands
I remember You arose from the dead
That I might have resurrection life

Invitation

Come come, come to the Savior alone
Into the presence of His throne
Kneel, kneel, kneel at His feet
Join in the fellowship sweet

Come, come, come to the Savior today
Let Him wash all your sins away
In His sweet presence abide
Casting all care and duty aside

Go, go, go forth in the fullness of His love
Giving glory to the Father above
Tell, tell, tellhow He has made you whole
Tell how He restores your soul

You Came To Me

I came to You in all my pain and suffering
I came to You in all my sin and wretchedness
I came to You, oh, Son of God
You died upon Calvary's cross
That I might be set free

You came to me in mercy and great love
You came to me with forgiveness from above
You came to me in faithfulness and truth
You came to me in righteousness
That I might be blameless in Your sight

I come to You just as I am
I come to You in faith and hope
I come to you in humility, in gratitude
I come to you, oh, Lamb of God
That You might be glorified

From The Holy Bible

*"For all have sinned and fall short of
the glory of God."Romans 3: 23*

*"For there is not a just man on earth
who does good and does not sin"
Ecclesiastes 7: 20*

*"For the wages of sin is death, but the
gift of God is eternal life in Christ
Jesus our Lord." Romans 6: 23*

*"For who ever calls upon the
name of the Lord shall be saved."
Romans 10: 13*

*"For God did not send His Son into
the world to condemn the world,
but that the world through Him
might be saved." John 3: 17*

Living in Christ

*"But grow in the grace and
knowledge of our
Lord and Savior,
Jesus Christ."II Peter 3: 18*

Believing

Believing, believing You, Lord
Believing You will do all You said You will do;
Your promises are true
Believing Youwill see me through

Trusting, trusting You, Jesus
Knowing that You will not depart
Leaning completely on Your grace
Looking to see You face to face

Loving, loving You, Lord
Loving You for all that You are
Loving You deep within my heart
Loving You enough to give You my all

Obeying, obeying You, my King
Obeying You is the key to victory
Growing each daymore maturity
Entering into all You have for me

Praising You, praising You Lord Jesus
You alone are worthy of all praise
Praising You with all my heart
Praising You in every circumstance of life

Serving, serving you, Lord
Your plans and purposes, not my own
When my life on earth is gone
Looking to hear You say,"Well done".

The Word Of Truth

Oh let Your Word be clear to me,
And let me not deceitful be,
But with child like faith draw near to You

Your Word of Truth will set me free,
Help me to understand what You say to me
That I might grow to maturity..to be like You

An understanding heart, O God;
In all that comes my way
I may follow You and not shrink back

The Word of the Lord is pure
The Word of the Lord is mighty
The Word of the Lord is powerful

The Word of the Lord brings healing
The Word of the Lord brings salvation
The Word of the Lord brings deliverance

Walking

I will walk by faith, not presumptuously,
Not in pride and self-glory
I will walk in the power of the Spirit
Not cowering in fear

I will walk in hope, not despair
Knowing Jesus is always there
I will walk in love, forgiveness,
Putting away anger, envy and resentment

I will walk in peace and rest
Knowing my Father gives what is best;
I will walk alert to the Spirit's voice
Enabling me to makethe right choice

Changing Me

What an awesome thing
that You the King of Kings
should dwell in my inner being.
Though with my natural eye
I can not always see or
know what is happening,
And though I may not always
feel your presence,
I know that You are changing me
Into Your very likeness

Getting To Know You

Getting to Know You
So many things on my mind
So many things to do
So many things to remember
So many plans to carry out
But above all this is

Getting to know You, Jesus
Getting to know You better
Getting to love You, Lord
Getting to love You more

Spending time alone in Your presence
Getting to know what is on Your mind
Willing to fulfill Your desire
Will make such a difference in my life

"For as the heavens are higher than the earth,
so are my ways higher than Your ways, and
Your thoughts than my thoughts."Isaiah 55:9

Standing

Standing in the presence of the Lord
Standing in the presence of His love
Standing in His power,
Standing in His might
Standing day and night
Jesus is my light

I do not stand alone
for You are with me
You are my refuge, my hiding place
My light in the dark, I will not be afraid
My hope in time of trouble,
My strength when I am weary

Jesus, I will stand for You
To You I will be true
I will not deny Your name
To You shall be all fame
By Your power divine
My faith shall not decline

The Battle Is The Lord's

I need not fight this battle alone;
It is the Lord who fights for me,
And He will be my guide;
He is ever at my side.

When I am weak, He is my strength;
In Him I find hope.
His Word will never fail;
His justice will prevail.

Fear may overtake me, but then I remember-
I am not in bondage again to fear;
But in Christ Jesus I have peace
In Him all turmoil must cease.

Dedication

"Blessed is the man who endures temptation; for when he has been approved, he will receive the crown of life which the Lord has promised to those that love Him."James 1: 12

Overcoming

To overcome worry and doubt
I cannot, but God can
Those little habits no one sees,
I cannot overcome, but God can
To have a truly repentant heart,
I cannot, but God can do it in me
To endure hardness as
a good soldier of Jesus Christ,
I cannot, but God can do it in me

I can no more keep myself saved,
than I can save myself
It is not about what I can do,
But what You, Lord,
can do through me
So I might as well quit trying
to do my very best
I might as well start yielding
and You will do the rest

I Am An Over-Comer

I want to overcome all self and sin
All pride and strife within
I want to overcome every obstacle
the enemy would put in the way
From all deception set free
I want to overcome all hate and fear
I want to overcome temptation near

In You, Lord, I am an over-comer
You have come to set me free
In You I have won the victory
You are the Mighty Conqueror
You have conquered sin and death
By Your precious blood You shed
You have crushed the enemy's head

Persevere

Persevere in faith, persevere in asking
Persevere in believing the answer is on the way

Persevere in kindness, Persevere in love
Persevere in gentleness through the Heavenly Dove

Persevere in temptations, persevere in afflictions
Persevere in grace until the victory is won

Persevere in justice, persevere in truth
Persevere in joy which follows obedience

Persevere in goodness, Persevere in giving
Persevere in serving, especially the household of faith

Persevere in patience, Persevere in meekness
Persevere in humility,In Christ's likeness you will be

There Are Those

There are those who do not turn back
from the labor and the heat of the day
through toil and tears
through stress and strain
in the harvest field they remain
The Father waits to greet them
with the words, "Well done."

There are those who will press on
to the goal of the prize of the King
In joyous rapture they sing
For they know that this life
with its sorrow and grief
compared to eternity is only so brief

There are those to whom Jesus is all
They have nothing of this world
to hold them back because
they have nothing left but Jesus

Continue On

I must continue on
this pathway of truth and light
neither turning to the left nor right
for soon there comes night
when no man can work
Continue in His love

I must continue on
this pathway of hope and faith
Though sadness fills my heart
when dear ones turned to error
depart no reproof to take heed
Continue in His truth

Though all would turn against me
and I am left to stand alone
Though some would scorn and ridicule
though I am frightened and intimidated
and my work goes unappreciated
Continue in His faith

Have I Denied?

Have I denied my Lord today?
To that question I would say-
"No, I would never You deny."
Yet, as I think upon my life-
I ponder in my heart,
What does it mean to deny my Lord?

He who lives in me will never leave
He desires that to Him I cleave;
He is the Lover of my soul.
How often do I tell Him so?
He waits to tell more about His grace
Have I denied Him fellowship?

There are so many things I find to do
To serve my Lord and others, too.
In the busyness of the day;
I try my best to fulfill the task-
My Savior says, "Why didn't you ask?"
Have I denied His order in my life?

I thank you, Lord, You are faithful
You cannot deny Yourself;
When I fall, You pick me up-
That I may learn Your ways;
So I pray that every day I will obey
Have I denied Your chastisement?

In this world of trials and temptations
I do not know what tomorrow holds-
Jesus, I thank You, You are in control.
When I stand before mere men
When I stand before Your throne
Help me to not deny Your name.

Am I Ready?

Am I ready to suffer for Your name?
Or would I rather sink back in shame?
Do I realize this is an opportunity
To share in Your suffering for me?
Counting it all joy that I am counted
worthy to suffer for Your name

My hands are Your hands
My feet are Your feet
My mouth is Yours to speak
When I am asked to sacrifice
To give my all and not count the price
Enable me to do it for You with joy

I need a vision, Lord, a purpose firm and true
Let not my vision be of selfish ambition
For then it would utterly fail
But I would look with Jesus unto the harvest
To share His shame and reproach

A Little Farther

The cost is not too deep, the journey is not too far
The way is not too hard
Just go a little farther, just love a little deeper
I cannot turn aside but in Your love abide
I must follow You Who will see me through

Each difficulty is an opportunity
to trust, to lean upon You
A challange to obey, to follow through
Be brave, be strong and of good courage
Go forward one step at a time

Submission

Not my will but Yours be done today
Not my plans but Yours be carried out, I pray

May the words I speak and the desires I seek
come from Your Spirit deep within my heart

I am not my own I am bought with the price
the precious blood of Jesus Christ
Above all else, I choose You

Following Jesus

Following Jesus, day after day
Following Jesus, He leads the way
Learning to listen to what He will say
Then by faith to trust and obey
If to His voice I will give heed
He will fulfill my every need

Following Jesus, there will be tests
He knows what is best
Though I may not always
see what is ahead
I must not be filled with fear and dread
He holds my hand never to let me go
In every trial He will bring me through

Who Are These?

Who are these, can they be counted?
Passing through the valley of Bacca
On their way to eternal bliss;
Faces uplifted to the Father,
Tear stained,
Showing pain,
Suffering shame for the Father's name
Homeless,
Lonely,
Wounded...just as you were , Lord

> I have a warm, cozy bed
> with plenty of covers over my head.
> They are shivering in prison cells
> no pillows for their heads
> with only cement floors for their beds
>
> If I am hungry to my cupboard I go
> a supply of food will be there, I know.
> In the refugee camps they lay
> many are starving every day.

I go to my closet to decide what to wear,
mix or match, I have such a choice.
Their clothes are tattered rags
with barely enough to cover their backs.

When I suffer bruises or breaks,
a trip to the doctor is all that it takes.
They are bruised from tortures sore
with no medicine on their wound to pour.

When I am lonely, many friends I can call
On any occasion
They sit alone in isolation

These are my brothers, these are my sisters
in Christ. This is my suffering family.
Jesus said, "In as much as you do it unto the
least of these my brethren, you do it unto me".

What gifts have I given to my "brethren" today?

Grace Alone

Saved by grace, and grace, alone
Faultless to stand before the throne
The gift of grace imparted
His will to do
That grace will never fail
Each trial to bring you through
His grace abounds in the gifts
He has given His church
to build up and strengthen
Called by grace to run the race
It will be worth it all
to gaze upon His face

Encouragement

"Be of good courage, and He shall strengthen your heart, all you that hope in the Lord."Psalm 31: 24

I'll Carry You Through

I'll carry you through the rocky path
I'll carry you through turbulent water
Across the desert, I will not leave you
Fear not, my child,
I'll carry you through

Though the way seems long
Though your heart grows weary
I hear your cry, I am near thee
Just trust in Me
to carry you through

You don't need to carry the burden
The responsibility is not yours
Leave all the details in My hand
I'll carry you through to the end

I Don't Need To Analyze

I don't need to analyze,
I just need to realize
that You are fully able, Lord
 to touch me and make me whole,
To believe that You are working
out Your purposes in my life
Bringing me to the place where
I realize that I can do nothing
in my own strength,

All that I am, all that I need
comes from you, Lord
I have so many ideas
of how it should be
But You know the beginning,
the end and everything between
What You choose to reveal is precious
Your thoughts are true,
Your Words are life

The Source Of My Joy

In all You are to me,
I lift up my hands to Thee
All that I ever could be
I owe to Thee
You are my strength
You are my joy, my life
When all resources fail
Help me to remember, Lord
You are my everything

The soure of my joy is
neither in my accomplishment
nor in my circumstance
The source of my joy
neither in popularity
nor in intellectuality
The source of my joy is
neither in what I possess
nor in my success
The source of my joy is
not in my own strength
I will rejoice in the Lord
I will joy in the God of my salvation

He Will Prevail

Thank you, Lord, You will prevail
Thank you, Lord, You never fail
You chase the clouds away
You turn my night to day
You have come in my heart to stay
In the spring rain or winter snow
The path that I take You know

I'll Never Walk Alone

I will never walk alone
Jesus walks beside me
He lives within me
He never will leave me or forsake me
Every day, every hour, every moment
He'll be with me
He knows the path before me
I'll never truly walk alone

Storm Clouds

When the storm clouds roll
and the NorthWind blows;
The rain drops come and
then the snow -
I surely know
My Father is in control.

So I will not fear
when the North Wind blows;
when the rain drops scatter
on my window pane and
the snow drifts come thick -
He holds me in the Hollow
of His hand.

When the storms of life
would overtake me
and disappointments
would overwhelm me,
Though I cannot see
abovethe clouds
My Father can see
the whole picture
And from His view
everything is all right.

There Is A Pathway

There's a pathway in the clouds for you
The Son of God is coming through
When there is darkness on every side
And your fears do not subside
He will make the darkness light
Who are ever in His sight

When your heart is filled with grief
And from pain there is no relief
Rest assured of His great love
He has sent the Heavenly Dove
The Comforter from above

Look Above

Look above earthy trials and problems
Above circumstances and feelings
Above imaginations and desires
Above all plans and ambitions

Look to Jesus, to His power,
Look to His strength
Look to His unfailing mercy
Look to His matchless love

Not Hidden From His Love

When circumstances
are beyond my control
When frustrations
mount up within my soul
and my own strength
is fragile and small

Then let me cry unto You, Lord
Let me come before Your presence
Feel the touch of Your compassion

When the tears stream down my face
Let me know they are not hidden
from Your love

Your understanding is infinite
Your mercies never fail
You are so real, so very real to me

Holy Spirit From Above

Holy Spirit from above
Come and fill your church with love
Springs of living water flow
That we might know
That fellowship so sweet
Of sitting at the Master's feet

Come Holy Spirit come
Sanctify your church today
Cleanse from all self and sin
Make us pure and whole within
Everyday and every hour
Come and fill us with your power
That we might spread the gospel seed
Reaching out to those in need

Come Gentle Dove
With your peace from above
Flooding my soul
Overflowing to all
Of Adam's race
That marvelous grace